Be a Space Scientist!

OUR SUN

CAN YOU FIGURE OUT ITS MYSTERIES?

David Hawksett

PowerKiDS
press

$$d = \sqrt{(x_2 - x_1) + (y_2 - y_1)^2}$$

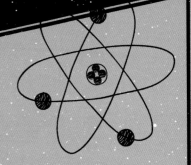

Published in 2018 by **The Rosen Publishing Group, Inc.**
29 East 21st Street, New York, NY 10010

Cataloging-in-Publication Data

Names: Hawksett, David.
Title: Our sun: can you figure out its mysteries? / David Hawksett.
Description: New York : PowerKids Press, 2018. | Series: Be a space scientist! | Includes index.
Identifiers: ISBN 9781538323007 (pbk.) | ISBN 9781538322079 (library bound) | ISBN 9781538323014 (6 pack)
Subjects: LCSH: Sun--Juvenile literature.
Classification: LCC QB521.5 H39 2018 | DDC 523.7--dc23

Produced for Rosen by Calcium
Editors for Calcium: Sarah Eason and Jennifer Sanderson
Designers for Calcium: Paul Myerscough and Jeni Child
Picture Researcher: Rachel Blount

Photo Credits: Cover: Shutterstock: Solarseven; Inside: Flickr: NASA Goddard Space Flight Center 30–31b; NASA: ESA&NASA/SoHO 25t, NASA/JPL/Space Science Institute 13b, NASA/SDO/Goddard Space Flight Center 27, 45tl; Shutterstock: Africa Studio 15l, Astrobobo 29t, Grisha Bruev 20, 44bl, Andrea Danti 8–9, 44tl, ERainbow 9r, Fluidworkshop 12–13, Hurst Photo 41r, Isak55 4–5, Ivannn 24–25, Petri Jauhiainen 30–31, Air Kanlaya 14–15, 44cl, Liseykina 38–39, Modigia 21, Mopic 36–37, Muratart 16–17, Romanova Natali 37r, Ningkub 10–11, Paulista 6–7, Sdecoret 1, 42, Sing5pan 7t, Robert Spriggs 40–41, 45bl, John T Takai 34b, Udaix 11t; Wikimedia Commons: Wolfgang Ellsässer 33l, Michael Franklin 33r, NASA 23t, 34–35, NASA/ESA/C.R. O'Dell (Vanderbilt University) 43, NASA Goddard Space Flight Center 18–19, NASA Goddard Space Flight Center/Image courtesy of Alan Friedman 22–23, NoobX (talk) 17b, Ferdianand Schmutzer 38b, Vacuum Tower Telescope 19b, Luc Viatour 28–29, Michel Wal 4b, Wellcome Images 32, 45cl.

Manufactured in China

CPSIA Compliance Information: Batch BW18PK: For Further Information contact Rosen Publishing, New York, New York at 1-800-237-9932.

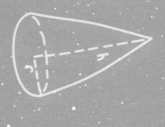

CONTENTS

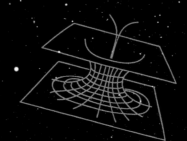

Chapter 1
EARTH'S SUN

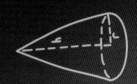

Ancient **civilizations** were fascinated by the night sky. They knew of four other planets in the **solar system**: Mercury, Venus, Mars, and Jupiter. These planets appeared as bright stars in the night sky, slowly changing their positions against the stars from night to night.

City of the Sun God

From at least 2613 BC, the ancient Egyptians worshiped the sun. They called it Ra and believed Ra ruled over all he had created. The sun symbolized light, warmth, and growth, making Ra the most important Egyptian god. From before 3100 BC, the ancient Egyptians established a city that was the center of worship of Atum, another god represented by the sun. The city was inhabited for nearly 3,000 years and was eventually known as Heliopolis, after the Greek sun god Helios. However, by the first century BC, Heliopolis was in ruins and without citizens.

Helios, the Greek version of the sun god, is the son of Hyperion and Theia. The Greeks imagined Helios driving a chariot across the sky, which moved as the sun rose and set from day to day.

> *Even close to sunset, when the sun is close to the **horizon**, our own star is dazzlingly bright. At sunset or sunrise, the light from the sun has to pass through more air to reach the ground than when it is high in the sky.*

The Sun at the Center

For many years, people followed the law of the Catholic Church and believed that the Earth, not the sun, was the center of the solar system. The astronomer Nicolaus Copernicus (1473–1543) challenged this view. He believed that the planets **rotated** around the sun. This is called the heliocentric, or "sun-centered," model of the solar system. In 1610, Galileo Galilei (1564–1642) used a newly invented **telescope** to look at the stars and planets. He discovered Jupiter's moons and proved that Copernicus's view was correct.

A Star

The first **philosopher** to suggest that the sun was a star was Anaxagoras in 450 BC, but the idea did not catch on. Much later, in 1590, Giordano Bruno (1548–1600) suggested the same thing, but was burned at the stake for it. Through the work of Copernicus and Galileo, the sun's place in the solar system became clear. Finally, in the nineteenth century, when astronomers could calculate the distances to stars and knew other things about them, they proved that the sun is a star.

$$d = \sqrt{(x_2 - x_1)^2 + (y_2 - y_1)^2}$$

DANGERS OF THE SUN

Even though the sun was worshiped by ancient civilizations, the people who lived then knew to never look at the sun directly. Today, we know that when we are facing in even roughly the same direction as the sun, our eyes will hurt even if we do not look directly at it. This is your body telling you to stop and look away from the dazzling light.

Do Not Do It!

As soon as you start to look at the sun, the surface of your eyeballs starts to develop sunburn. This is a result of the powerful **ultraviolet (UV)** light the sun gives out. Our eyes cannot see ultraviolet light, but it is what causes skin to blister and burn even after a short time. The UV light will make the outer layers of your eyeballs blister and crack, but you will not feel the pain from it until hours later.

This telescope is pointing in the right direction, at the night sky! If you were to point it at the sun and look through it, you could suffer from instant blindness.

$$d = \sqrt{(x_2 - x_1)^2 + (y_2 - y_1)^2}$$

At the start or end of a total **eclipse** of the sun, the edge of the sun can be seen, here at the upper right. Even this tiny portion of the sun can damage your eyes.

Sun Dangers

If you stare at the sun for more than just a few seconds, you will seriously damage your eyes. Permanent damage to your eyesight can happen in less than one minute, but even looking at the sun for a few seconds at a time can damage your eyes over time. When a total eclipse of the sun happened in 1999, some people in England went to see their doctors after watching it without eye protection. Around half of these people had permanent eyesight loss.

Looking at the Sun Safely

The only way to look at the sun safely is by using **eclipse glasses**. These cut out the harmful UV light and make the sun dim enough to be seen without pain. You should never make your own eclipse glasses, but instead ask a responsible adult to help you buy a safe, high-quality pair.

SPLITTING LIGHT

$$d = \sqrt{(x_2 - x_1) + (y_2 - y_1)^2}$$

Most people believe that sunlight is yellow, because when the sun is high in the sky, at around midday, it appears yellow. At sunset or sunrise, when the sun is low on the horizon, it looks much more orange and red. If you could go into space and look at the sun safely without damaging your eyes, you would notice that it is actually white.

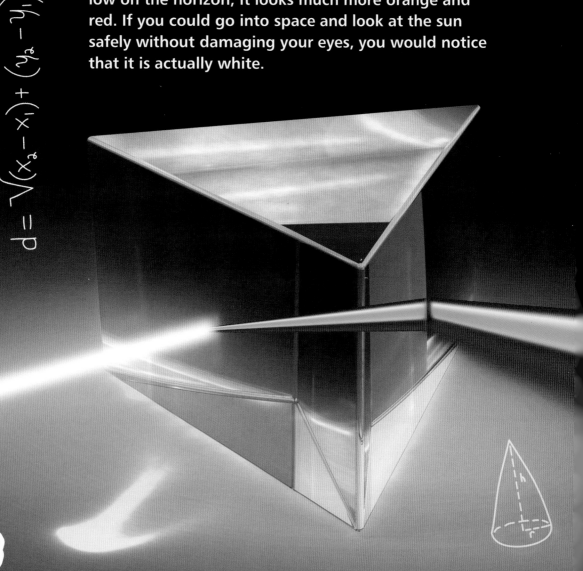

A Mixture of Colors

You can use a simple scientific device called a **prism** to split sunlight up into its ingredients. A prism is usually made of glass and is see-through. When you hold a prism up to the sun, its light enters the prism and comes out the other side. When light enters a see-through substance that has a different **density** from what it was in before, it is bent. As the sunlight comes out the other side, the light forms a **rainbow** of colors. sunlight is actually made up of all these colors mixed together.

When light is split by a glass prism, you can see that red light is bent the least and violet is bent the most. Combining all these colors together makes pure white light.

Be a Space Scientist!

The easiest way to see sunlight split up is to let nature do it for us. If the sun is out while it is raining, we see a rainbow in the sky. Each falling raindrop acts as a tiny prism. The sunlight enters the raindrop and some of it is reflected back to us. When it bounces off the inside of the raindrop, the sunlight is bent, like in a prism, and the different colors are bent differently. You can make your own rainbow with a garden hose. Face away from the sun and spray the hose so that tiny water droplets form a mist. A mini rainbow should appear.

You can make a partial arc of a rainbow with a garden hose. If you spray the water higher in the air, you can sometimes make a circular rainbow.

Chapter 2
THE SPECTRUM

Light travels through air and space as a wave. Bigger waves have more energy, which makes them brighter. To understand this, think of ocean waves. Higher wave crests, or tops, have more **energy**, just like higher light waves have brighter light. The distance between the waves is called **wavelength**. It determines the color of the light. While the waves on the ocean can be hundreds of feet apart, light waves are much closer together.

The waves on the ocean move through the water in the same way waves of light move through space or anything see-through.

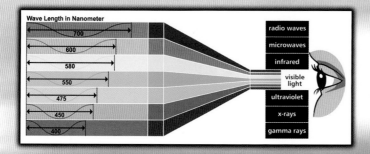

Wave Length in Nanometer

700
600
580
550
475
450
400

radio waves
microwaves
infrared
visible light
ultraviolet
x-rays
gamma rays

To remember the correct order of the colors of the visible spectrum, some people remember "Roy G. Biv," which stands for red, orange, yellow, green, blue, indigo, violet.

$$d = \sqrt{(x_2 - x_1) + (y_2 - y_1)^2}$$

A Nanometer

Light waves are so close together, a new metric unit of measurement is used to describe them. A meter-long ruler is split into 100 centimeters. Each centimeter is split into 10 millimeters, and these are the smallest divisions you can see on the ruler. If you then divided each millimeter a million times, you would get one nanometer. A typical human hair is around 75,000 nanometers across. The distance between the tops of the waves in visible light depends on the light's color. With red light, the waves are 650 nanometers apart. This is the longest wavelength of light we can see. Violet-colored light has a wavelength of just 400 nanometers and is the shortest wavelength we can see.

The Full Spectrum

When sunlight is split into its colors, it is described as a "**spectrum** of light." This really means the range of light we can see, from the lowest to highest wavelength. However, the true spectrum does not stop there. Beyond red, moving into longer wavelengths, is **infrared radiation**, which is felt as heat. **Radio waves** have even longer wavelengths, where the distances between each wave can range from 0.03 inch (1 mm) to more than 62 miles (100 km). On the other end of the spectrum, beyond violet, is harmful UV light. Then there are even more harmful **X-rays** and **gamma rays**. All of these different wavelengths together are called the electromagnetic spectrum.

THE SUN'S HEAT

The most obvious feature of our sun is its brightness, so remember not to look at the sun. Sunlight also contains heat energy. As soon as we step into the sunlight, we feel its heat on our skin. This is the invisible infrared radiation that our eyes have not **evolved** to be sensitive to. The heat from the sun drives life on Earth. Plants use sunlight as a source of energy to help them grow and to convert **carbon dioxide** to **oxygen**. This process is known as **photosynthesis**, and without it there would be no plants – and no plant-eating animals.

$$d = \sqrt{(x_2 - x_1) + (y_2 - y_1)^2}$$

Mercury

Venus

Earth

Mars

Jupiter

Saturn

Uranus

Neptune

The planets in the solar system beyond Mars are all very cold, which is why many of their moons are made mostly of ice.

How Hot — How Far?

The amount of heat Earth receives from the sun is a result of its distance from it. Mercury and Venus, which are closer to the sun than Earth, receive more infrared from the sun, so they are hotter. Mars and the **outer planets** are farther away, so they are colder than Earth. This table of the solar system shows the planets with their distances from the sun and their average temperatures.

PLANET	DISTANCE FROM SUN	TEMPERATURE
Mercury	36 million miles (58 million km)	-275–840°F (-171–449°C)
Venus	67.2 million miles (108 million km)	870°F (466°C)
Earth	93 million miles (150 million km)	45°F (7°C)
Mars	141.6 million miles (228 million km)	-195–70°F (-126–21°C)
Jupiter	483.6 million miles (778 million km)	-244°F (-153°C)
Saturn	886.7 million miles (1,427 million km)	-300°F (-184°C)
Uranus	1,784 million miles (2,870 million km)	-300°F (-184°C)
Neptune	2,794 million miles (4,496 million km)	-370°F (-223°C)

Trapping and Reflecting Heat

As you can see, Venus is hotter than Mercury despite being farther from the sun. Venus's thick **atmosphere** traps heat from the sun. Mercury cannot trap heat because it does not have an atmosphere. The temperature of a planet or moon also depends on how reflective it is. The sun heats dark worlds more than bright ones because the brighter ones reflect more of the heat back into space. The same effect occurs if two identical objects are painted, one black and one white, and put in sunlight. The black object will become hotter than the white one. In space, this effect is illustrated by Saturn's moon Enceladus. Enceladus is covered in ice and reflects more than 90% of its sunlight back into space.

Saturn's small, icy moon, Enceladus, is the most reflective object in the solar system. Its patterns of grooves are believed to be caused by volcanoes deep under the ice.

UV DETECTION

UV light was discovered in 1801. **Physicist** Johann Wilhelm Ritter (1776–1810) was experimenting with a chemical called silver chloride, which turns dark when exposed to light. Ritter noticed that something he could not see was darkening the silver chloride more than violet light did. He realized there must be invisible rays at work, with higher energy than violet light. He called these rays UV light.

Seeing UV Light

Our eyes cannot see UV light, but some animals can. For example, reindeer have evolved to see some UV light, which helps them spot polar bears. The bears are difficult to see against the white snow, but they do show up in UV light.

Bees are one of many insects that can see UV light. Many flowers have patterns in their petals that attract bees and can be seen only in UV light.

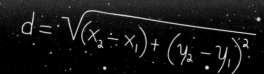

$$d = \sqrt{(x_2 - x_1) + (y_2 - y_1)^2}$$

Be a Space Scientist!

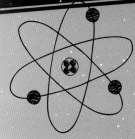

Just as we can feel heat to detect infrared, there are ways to detect UV light.

You Will Need

- 2 see-through glasses
- Tap water
- Tonic water
- 2 paper labels
- A pen
- A black sheet of paper
- A hardcover book
- A dark room
- A flashlight
- A sunny day

Instructions

1. Fill one glass or cup with tap water, and the other one with tonic water. Use the pen and the labels to mark the contents of each cup.

2. Place the sheet of paper against the book and prop it up so it stands upright. Look through each cup to see the black paper behind.

3. In a dark room, shine the flashlight into the cups of liquid while looking through them at the black paper. What happens? Do the tonic water and tap water look the same?

4. On a sunny day, take all your equipment outside. Place the upright book with black paper on a surface that is facing toward the sun.

5. Look through the cups so you can see the black paper. What happens now? Can you see a difference between the appearance of the two liquids in sunlight?

Chapter 3
THE SUN'S SURFACE

Chinese and Korean astronomers were instructed by their **emperors** to try to observe details on the sun. In the Chinese *Book of Changes*, published in around 800 BC, dark marks on the sun's surface were recorded. In 300 BC, the first recorded mention of one of these dark markings appeared in Western literature. In AD 807, a monk noted a large, dark spot on the sun that was visible for eight days.

Strange Horns and Dark Spots

The ancient Babylonians recorded eclipses in the eighth century BC. A solar eclipse is when the moon passes between the sun and Earth. Strange features on the sun's surface had been recorded during eclipses of the sun since ancient times. Later, in 1185, it was noted in the Russian *Chronicle of Novgorod*, "The sun became similar to the moon and from its horns came out live embers." These "horns" could be seen only during an eclipse.

$$d = \sqrt{(x_2 - x_1) + (y_2 - y_1)^2}$$

The other type of eclipse is a lunar eclipse. In these eclipses, it is Earth that passes between the sun and the moon, temporarily blocking sunlight from the lunar surface.

The Helioscope

After the invention of the telescope in the seventeenth century, astronomers devised a way of looking at the sun safely. If an astronomer points a telescope at the sun and looks through it, the concentrated magnified light will blind their eyes right away. However, if they hold a sheet of paper to the eyepiece and move it away by about 1 foot (30 cm), what is seen though the telescope is projected onto the paper. Using this idea, Christoph Scheiner (1573–1650) invented a special telescope called a helioscope in the early seventeenth century. Galileo then improved the design. The helioscope allowed astronomers to see the dark "sunspots" on the sun's surface in detail for the first time.

The McMath-Pierce telescope was built in 1962 in Arizona and for many years was the largest telescope in the world designed to study the sun.

WHAT CAN WE SEE?

To get a clear view of the sun, astronomers take photographs using cameras attached to telescopes so that they do not have to look at the sun. What are these astronomers looking at?

On August 31, 2012, astronomers captured this image showing a massive eruption of material from the sun.

A New Type of Matter

Everything in the universe can be divided into energy and **matter**. Energy is all the light, heat, UV, radio waves, X-rays, and gamma rays. Matter is all the actual stuff: planets, stars, gas, dust, people, and anything that weighs something. On Earth, there are three types of matter: solids, liquids, and gases. Matter can exist in any of these forms, depending on the conditions around it. For example, water can be liquid, gas as water vapor in the air, and solid in the form of ice. However, there is a fourth type of matter that does not exist naturally on Earth. If you heat a solid, it eventually melts into a liquid and then **evaporates** into a gas. If the gas is heated enough, it then turns into plasma. The sun and all the other stars are made from plasma. When astronomers look at the sun, they see the top layer of glowing plasma.

Granules on the Sun

When a pot of soup is boiled, patterns moving on the surface can be seen. When a gas or liquid is heated, it expands (becomes bigger) and becomes less dense and rises. In 1861, James Nasmyth (1808–1890) discovered details on the sun much smaller than the giant dark sunspots. These features, which are now known as granules, cover the whole sun. The granules are around 930 miles (1,497 km) across but they last only up to 20 minutes before vanishing and being replaced by new ones. These changing patterns result from hot plasma rising from below, just like the patterns on the boiling soup.

The individual granules on the sun can be seen in this image. They look like small bright blobs with darker borders. The large feature in the center is a sunspot.

$$d = \sqrt{(x_2 - x_1) + (y_2 - y_1)^2}$$

SEEING THE SUN

As people must NEVER look at the sun, to see some of the features safely, they use special eclipse glasses or a helioscope, like Galileo. They can also make a device called a pinhole camera to look at the sun.

Using eclipse glasses is the only way to look directly at the sun without damaging your eyesight. Here an eclipse of the sun by the moon is underway. The moon is covering about half of the sun, making the sun look like a crescent.

Pinhole Cameras

A pinhole camera is the simplest kind of camera you can make. When light passes through a small enough hole, it can project an upside-down version of an image on the other side. It is one of the properties of light that allows this to happen. Pinhole cameras can be built inside dark boxes to make an image clearer, but the simplest form of pinhole camera is all you need to see the sun.

$$d = \sqrt{(x_2 - x_1) + (y_2 - y_1)^2}$$

Be a Space Scientist!

Why not make your own pinhole camera to safely take a closer look at the sun? What can you see?

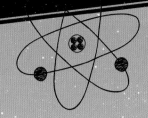

You Will Need

- 2 sheets of white card stock
- Scissors
- Tape
- A pin or needle
- Aluminum foil
- A sunny day

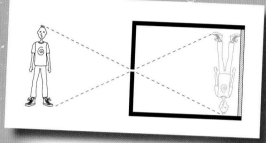

*The nature of light causes the images you project with your pinhole camera to be upside-down. When you project the sun, your image will show the sun's south **pole** at the top, instead of the bottom.*

Instructions

1. Take one of your sheets of card stock and cut a square hole in the center. The hole should be a few inches across.

2. Cut out a piece of the foil slightly larger than the hole you cut in the card stock. Use the tape to stick the foil over the hole. Then use the needle or pin to make a tiny hole right in the center of the foil. This is your pinhole camera.

3. Go outside on a sunny day and put your second sheet of card stock on the ground. Stand facing the second sheet with the sun behind you. Make sure the card stock is not in your shadow.

4. Hold up your first card stock with the foil and the pinhole so that it casts a shadow on the card stock on the ground. You should be able to see a fairly dim, white circle. This is the sun projected through the pinhole. The narrow beam of light that the hole allowed to pass through the aluminum has spread out to show the disk of the sun. It will not show much detail, but if there are large sunspots present, you may be able to see them projected onto the second piece of card stock.

Chapter 4
THE SUN'S SPOTS

Dark spots on the surface of the sun were the first detail ever seen on our star. The biggest sunspots are even visible to the naked eye, but remember not to look at the sun. They exist on the **photosphere** of the sun, which is the bright surface seen from Earth. The dark spots range in size from around 10 to 100,000 miles (16–160,934 km) across. They can last from a few days to several months before they disappear.

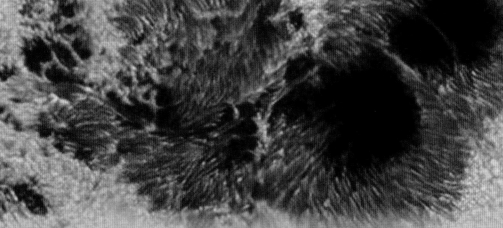

In July 2012, a giant group of sunspots was seen on the surface of the sun. The largest spot shown in this image was larger than 11 Earths.

Hot or Cold?

Sunspots are black, so some people think they are cold. However, they are actually very hot. The temperature of a sunspot is between 4,890 and 7,590°F (2,699 and 4,199°C) but because the rest of the sun's surface is around 9,930°F (5,499°C), they appear dark in comparison. They have two parts – the darker central **umbra** and the lighter outer **penumbra**.

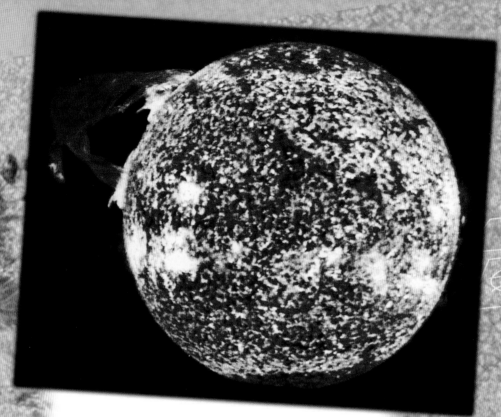

On December 19, 1973, astronauts on the National Aeronautics and Space Administration (NASA) Skylab space station photographed one of the biggest storms ever seen on the sun. This giant loop of plasma was more than 365,000 miles (587,411 km) across.

Sunspots and Storms

Above the sun's photosphere, massive storms and eruptions are visible. Solar flares are huge erupting storms that send clouds of electrically charged **atoms** into space. The biggest solar flares erupt with around 20 million times the energy of the most powerful **nuclear weapon** ever tested on Earth. The clouds of atoms and **electrons** can reach Earth, and because they are electrically charged, they can disrupt electrical power on Earth. In 1859, Richard Carrington (1826–1875) and Richard Hodgson (1804–1872) first recorded these storms. A few days after Carrington witnessed a giant white flare on the side of the sun, **telegraph** communications in North America and Europe failed as a storm hit Earth. This was one of the biggest solar flares ever seen, and a similar event today could knock out electrical systems and communications satellites around the world. Astronomers studying the sun have all noticed one thing: flares and other types of **solar activity** seem to happen when there are many sunspots on the sun's surface.

LEARNING FROM SUNSPOTS

Since the invention of the telescope in the early seventeenth century, astronomers have been watching the dark spots on the sun. The sunspots could be seen changing size and shape, and disappearing altogether, but they also seemed to move across the face of the sun. The fact that they all moved in the same direction, from left to right as seen from Earth, suggested the sun was rotating.

The Sun Spins

Everything in the solar system rotates, and so the discovery that the sun also spins on its axis was not a surprise. The sun and planets formed from the same spinning disk of dust and gas, so the sun spins in the same direction that the planets move in their **orbits**. However, the sun does not spin at a constant speed. Astronomers have discovered that spots on the sun's **equator** take 25 days to spin around once, while spots near the poles take 36 days to spin around once. This is because the sun is made of plasma and is not solid.

This image shows solar maximum. The dark red and black areas are sunspots.

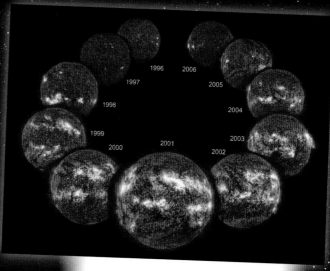

1996 2006
1997 2005
1998 2004
1999 2003
2000 2001 2002

This sequence shows a solar cycle (see below). The sun at its solar maximum is at the front and solar minimum is at the back.

$$d = \sqrt{(x_2 - x_1)^2 + (y_2 - y_1)^2}$$

Seasons on the Sun

By the second half of the seventeenth century, sunspot watchers were out of luck. Sunspots hardly appeared, and it seemed something about the sun had changed. This went against teachings by the Catholic Church that all astronomical objects were perfect and unchanging. Now that 400 years have passed since the invention of the telescope, modern astronomers have 400 years of historical observations to compare. The sun, it seems, has seasons of its own. Every 11 years, the number of sunspots reaches its highest, and in between, they can disappear completely. This is known as a solar cycle. The more sunspots there are, the more flares and other solar storms occur. We call this solar maximum. When there are few sunspots, flares, and solar storms, it is solar minimum.

DIFFERENT SUNS?

Our eyes can see only the tiny part of the electromagnetic spectrum we call visible light, but the sun does not shine just in visible light. We have seen that it also shines in UV and infrared. It actually shines across the whole spectrum, giving out natural radio waves and X-rays, too. Not all of this range of radiation even reaches the ground. Some of it is reflected back into space by our upper atmosphere. To get a perfect view of the sun, we have to get above our atmosphere and into space.

The Sun Across the Spectrum

The Solar & Heliospheric Observatory (SOHO) mission was launched in 2005 and is still in operation. SOHO orbits the sun and has been studying our star in different wavelengths.

$$d = \sqrt{(x_2 - x_1) + (y_2 - y_1)^2}$$

Be a Space Scientist!

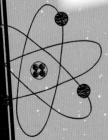

The 12 pictures of the sun shown on the next page were taken by a NASA sun orbiter called the **Solar Dynamics Observatory (SDO)**. The second image from the right on the top row (3) is taken in the visible light we can see. The only detail we can see are some large groups of sunspots. The rest of the images were taken at different wavelengths that our eyes cannot see. Second from the left on the top row (2) is a black and white image that shows a map of magnetism on the sun's surface. The most magnetic areas show up as bright and dark markings. What do you notice about the black and white markings on image 2 when you compare it with image 3?

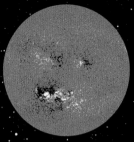

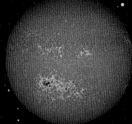

1. HMI Dopplergram
Surface movement
Photosphere

2. HMI Magnetogram
Magnetic field

3. HMI Continuum
Visible light

4. 7,600°F
(4,204°C)
Photosphere

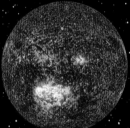

5. 17,600°F
(9,760°C)
Photosphere

6. 90,000°F
(49,982°C)
Photosphere

7. 1,080,000°F
(599,982°C)
Photosphere

8. 1,800,000°F
(999,983°C)
Corona/flare plasma

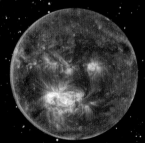

9. 3,600,000°F
(1,999,982°C)
Active regions

10. 4,500,000°F
(2,499,982°C)
Active regions

11. 10,800,000°F
(444,427°C)
Flaring regions

12. 18,000,000°F
(9,999,982°C)
Flaring regions

All the colors shown in these photographs are false. They are all actually black and white. SDO scientists use different colors to help show the wavelengths they are looking at when they look at different images of the sun. All 12 pictures were taken at the same time and highlight temperature differences on the sun.

Chapter 5
ECLIPSES OF THE SUN

Like all planets, Earth orbits the sun. The moon orbits Earth, taking around a month to go around Earth. This is where the word "month" comes from. This means that once a month, the moon passes between the sun and Earth. However, the moon's orbit is inclined to Earth's orbit around the sun. Imagine Earth orbiting the sun on the surface of a flat lake. The moon's orbit takes it under water for half the time and in the air the other half. This means that the moon passes directly in front of the sun only occasionally. Then we have a solar eclipse.

A total solar eclipse occurred in August 1999 and was visible from parts of Europe. Here the surface of the sun is completely hidden.

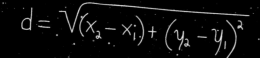

$$d = \sqrt{(x_2 - x_1) + (y_2 - y_1)^2}$$

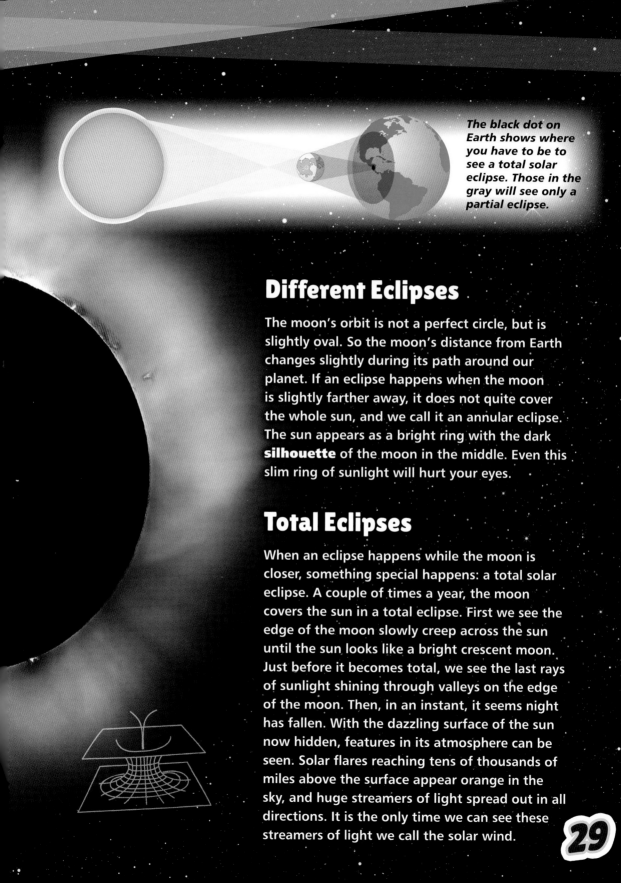

The black dot on Earth shows where you have to be to see a total solar eclipse. Those in the gray will see only a partial eclipse.

Different Eclipses

The moon's orbit is not a perfect circle, but is slightly oval. So the moon's distance from Earth changes slightly during its path around our planet. If an eclipse happens when the moon is slightly farther away, it does not quite cover the whole sun, and we call it an annular eclipse. The sun appears as a bright ring with the dark **silhouette** of the moon in the middle. Even this slim ring of sunlight will hurt your eyes.

Total Eclipses

When an eclipse happens while the moon is closer, something special happens: a total solar eclipse. A couple of times a year, the moon covers the sun in a total eclipse. First we see the edge of the moon slowly creep across the sun until the sun looks like a bright crescent moon. Just before it becomes total, we see the last rays of sunlight shining through valleys on the edge of the moon. Then, in an instant, it seems night has fallen. With the dazzling surface of the sun now hidden, features in its atmosphere can be seen. Solar flares reaching tens of thousands of miles above the surface appear orange in the sky, and huge streamers of light spread out in all directions. It is the only time we can see these streamers of light we call the solar wind.

AURORAE AND THE SOLAR WIND

When the British astronomer Richard Carrington first saw a solar flare in 1859, it led him to believe that the sun sent out a steady "wind" of particles into space. **Comets** are chunks of ice and dust left over from the formation of the sun and planets. Most have very long oval orbits that bring them into the **inner solar system**. The heat from the sun makes the ice start to evaporate into a gas. This erupting gas takes dust from the surface with it as it spews into space. This gas and dust gets stretched into a long tail millions of miles long, but the tail is not always behind the comet. Instead it always points away from the sun. In 1947, German astronomer Ludwig Biermann (1907–1986) suggested it was this wind from the sun that pushed the gas and dust away, forming the comet's tail.

A Shrinking Sun?

The solar wind is made up of electrically charged particles that are emitted mainly from the sun's equatorial (middle) regions. These tiny particles travel at speeds between 155 and 460 miles per second (249 and 740 km/s). Around 2 billion pounds (907,185 metric tons) of mass are lost from the sun every single second as a result of the solar wind. This adds up to the sun losing the same mass as Earth every 150 million years. This may sound like a lot, but over the course of the sun's 4.6-billion-year life so far, only one-hundredth of one percent of it has been emitted as solar wind.

$$d = \sqrt{(x_2 - x_1) + (y_2 - y_1)^2}$$

The Aurora

When the solar wind hits Earth, the electrically charged particles interact with Earth's **magnetic field**. This funnels the particles away from Earth's equator so that they form a ring at the north and south poles. As these fast, charged particles hit the upper atmosphere at the poles, it makes the air glow. If you are close to the polar regions, you can see this happen in the night sky as a spectacular light show known as the aurora. It is the same kind of process that makes a neon light tube glow when it has electricity running through it, but it is also the best evidence for the existence of the solar wind.

This artist's impression shows Earth being protected by its invisible magnetic field. Charged particles stream toward Earth's poles where the magnetic field is weakest.

IN TRANSIT

The planets Mercury and Venus are closer to the sun than Earth. This means they, like the moon, pass between the sun and us. Also like the moon, their orbits are slightly inclined to ours, so Mercury or Venus passing across the face of the sun is quite rare. We call these events transits, and they occur in predictable patterns. Mercury transits across the sun around 13 times each century. Transits of Venus are much more uncommon. It happens twice, eight years apart, and then there are gaps of 121.5 and 105.5 years before the pattern repeats.

$$d = \sqrt{(x_2 - x_1)^2 + (y_2 - y_1)^2}$$

Today, transits of Venus and Mercury are observed by astronomers around the world. But in 1639, only the astronomers Jeremiah Horrocks and William Crabtree (see opposite) measured the transit of Venus.

Be a Space Scientist!

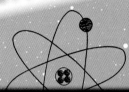

Mercury is the smallest planet in the solar system. During a transit of Mercury across the sun, the planet is around 48 million miles (77.2 million km) from Earth. During a transit of Venus across the sun, Venus is around 25 million miles (40.2 million km) from Earth. Using this information, can you tell whether planet A is Venus or Mercury?

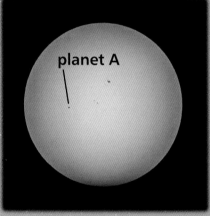

planet A

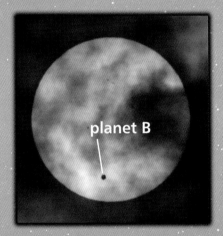

planet B

Measuring the Solar System

Venus takes several hours to cross the face of the sun during a rare transit. In the seventeenth century, astronomers realized they could use a transit of Venus to measure the solar system. This is how it worked: Two British astronomers, Jeremiah Horrocks (1618–1641) and William Crabtree (1610–1644) both set up their telescopes to project an image of the sun. A transit of Venus was predicted for December 4, 1639. Both astronomers watched Venus transit the sun and measured its precise path. However, Horrocks and Crabtree were around 30 miles (48 km) away from each other, meaning they watched the transit from slightly different angles. This made their timings of the transit slightly different and they were able to use their results to estimate the distance to the sun. Their result, 59.4 million miles (95.6 million km), was around two-thirds of the actual distance, but it was more accurate than previous estimates.

Chapter 6

INSIDE THE SUN

Our sun has no solid surface anywhere on it or inside it. Compared to Earth and the other planets, it is immense — 109 Earths could be lined up across its face and 1,300,000 Earths could fit inside it! In the very center of the sun is its core, where all the sun's energy is created. The core reaches about a quarter of the way from the middle to the surface.

Layering of the sun

inner core

radiative zone

convection zone

subsurface flows

photosphere

chromosphere

corona

This diagram shows the different layers of the sun with its core in the middle. The surface of the sun that we can see is the photosphere.

The Radiative Zone

Above the core is a region known as the radiative zone. It extends to around three-quarters of the way to the surface. It becomes less dense as you travel outward. At the bottom of this zone, close to the core, the plasma that makes up the sun is about as dense as gold. This means that if you held some in your hand, it would weigh the same as gold. At the top of this zone, though, the plasma's density has dropped to around one-fifth that of water. The energy created in the core is released as light and other radiation. Traveling at the speed of light, 186,282 miles per second (299,792 km/s), this radiation keeps bouncing around, taking a very indirect path to the surface, where it can escape into space. This radiation can stay trapped in the sun for millions of years.

The Convection Zone

Above the radiative zone is the convection zone. Here the plasma moves like a pot of boiling soup. Plasma at the top of the radiative zone carries heat upward to cooler regions before sinking again. This zone reaches all the way to the visible surface, and the effect of this movement can be seen as solar granules. By the time you reach the surface, or photosphere, the plasma is very thin. Its density is only around one ten-thousandth of Earth's atmosphere.

This solar flare erupted in March 2012. This year was close to solar maximum and saw a lot of activity on the sun, including flares and sunspots.

$$d = \sqrt{(x_2 - x_1) + (y_2 - y_1)^2}$$

THE CORE

$$d = \sqrt{(x_2 - x_1) + (y_2 - y_1)^2}$$

When the sun and planets formed from a cloud of gas and dust in space, they became hot in their centers. This was because of the weight of all the material around it, squeezing in on the centers. You can demonstrate this by holding your thumb over the end of a bicycle pump and trying to pump it. The air inside heats up just as the centers of planets and stars do.

The Center of the Sun

The main difference between a planet and a star is that the center of the star became hot enough for nuclear reactions to begin. The temperature in the sun's core is around 27 million °F (15 million °C). The sun is mostly hydrogen, the lightest and most common **element** in the universe. Each hydrogen atom has a central **proton**, which carries a positive electrical charge. Orbiting this proton is a negatively charged electron. In a plasma, the protons constantly swap their electrons with their neighbors. Opposite charges attract and similar charges repel, just like when you try to stick two magnets together. As protons are all positively charged, they are forced to keep their distance from each other.

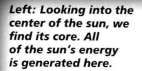

Left: Looking into the center of the sun, we find its core. All of the sun's energy is generated here.

*Right: When a nuclear bomb explodes, it converts hydrogen to **helium**, just like in the sun, and the energy is released as an enormous explosion.*

Changing Hydrogen into Helium

Along with its extreme heat, the sun's core also experiences enormous pressure. It is impossible to measure it directly. Astronomers believe the pressure in the center, or how much you would be squeezed by the weight of all the plasma above you, is around 260 billion times what you feel on Earth's surface. These conditions are enough to overcome the charge on the protons. Instead of repelling each other, they **fuse** together, changing from hydrogen into helium. As they fuse together, enormous amounts of energy are released. It is this energy that makes the sun, and all the other stars, shine so brightly.

How Long Will the Sun Last?

In the sun's core, around 661 million tons (600 million tonnes) of hydrogen are fused into helium every second. However, the helium produced is only 657 million tons (596 million tonnes). So around 4.4 million tons (4 million tonnes) every second are converted to pure energy. It may sound like a lot, but the sun is big and has enough hydrogen **fuel** to last another 5 billion years or so.

Almost all life on Earth is driven by the sun. Plants use their leaves to soak up sunlight. They take in carbon dioxide and give out oxygen. This process keeps Earth's atmosphere suitable for animals, which breathe in the oxygen and breathe out carbon dioxide into the air.

$$d = \sqrt{(x_2 - x_1) + (y_3 - y_1)^2}$$

WHAT IS EQUILIBRIUM?

The nuclear fusion that happens in the sun's core is the same process as in a hydrogen bomb. Unlike the bomb, the sun does not explode. Instead, it continues to shine. To understand why this happens, we need to know what equilibrium is. Equilibrium is about things being in balance. Imagine a tug of war between two teams that are equally strong. When they are both pulling at their hardest, the rope becomes tight but does not move. Both teams stay still because the **force** of each team balances out the other.

The sun's energy pushes outward while its **gravity** pulls inward, keeping everything in balance.

Be a Space Scientist!

We can demonstrate why the sun does not explode by showing that it is in equilibrium.

If you blow up a balloon, you make the **air pressure** inside higher than the air pressure outside. The high-pressure air pushes against the inside of the balloon's rubber skin and forces it to expand. At the same time, rubber squeezes back, trying to make the balloon smaller. The air's push and the rubber's squeezing find a balance where they exert exactly the same amount of force. In other words, the balloon is in equilibrium as both forces balance each other.

In the sun, the energy from the nuclear fusion is pushing outward, like in an explosion. However, the sun is heavy, so it has enough gravity to contain the explosion. The sun is in equilibrium, with its gravity trying to make it smaller, while its energy tries to make it bigger. Can you see how this relates to the balloon?

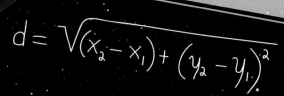

$$d = \sqrt{(x_2 - x_1) + (y_2 - y_1)^2}$$

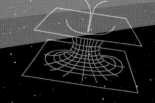

THE SUN'S FATE

Stars much bigger than the sun end their lives in spectacular explosions known as **supernovae**. Smaller stars, like the sun, end their lives in a much more gentle, but still spectacular way. In 1764, the French astronomer Charles Messier (1730–1817) conducted a survey of the night sky. He was interested in the clouds of gas and dust, or nebulae, which had been seen through telescopes. Messier found that some of these nebulae looked like planets through a telescope. William Herschel (1738–1822), the astronomer who discovered Uranus, was the first to call called them planetary nebulae.

Running Low on Fuel

In around five billion years, the sun will start to run out of its hydrogen fuel, having converted most of it to helium in its core. It will start giving out less energy, upsetting the equilibrium with gravity, and its core will start to shrink. This will make the helium hot enough to start a new nuclear fusion reaction in which it turns into another element, **carbon**. Some of this carbon will fuse with more helium to make oxygen. All the oxygen and carbon in the universe was made in the cores of stars in this way.

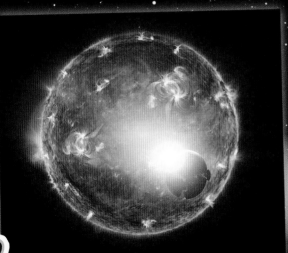

Five billion years from now, the sun will swell to many times its original size. It will become cooler and redder, but its expansion will mean it is much closer to Earth.

$$d = \sqrt{(x_2 - x_1) + (y_2 - y_1)^2}$$

The Helix Nebula is an expanding shell of gas and dust that used to be a star like our sun.

The End of Earth

At this stage, the sun will swell up dramatically. It will grow from being a normal star to being a **red giant**. It will engulf Earth and all the inner planets and destroy them completely. Its outer layers will slowly drift off into space in an expanding shell of gas. Left behind will be the naked core of the sun, no longer making new elements, but still shining white due to the heat it already had in it from when it was fusing elements together. This core is now known as a white dwarf star. It will be around the size of Earth and will take billions of years to cool down and stop shining. The outer layers, as they drift outward, will become a beautiful planetary nebula, just like those Messier discovered.

BE A SPACE SCIENTIST! ANSWERS

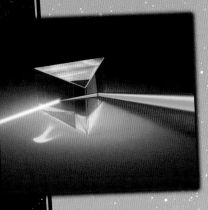

8-9 Splitting Light

Congratulations! You made a rainbow. But why did your mini rainbow keep shining despite the drops of rain falling as a result of gravity? From a distance, you cannot see the individual raindrops. As one falls, another raindrop from above replaces it. Each drop acts like a prism, and because there are so many of them, you see the rainbow shine continuously.

14-15 UV Detection

Indoors using a flashlight, both liquids look the same. However, the tonic water contains chemicals that are sensitive to UV light. Outdoors, the tonic water will look slightly blue compared with the normal water. This means tonic water can be used as a UV light detector, and you can prove that the sun gives out UV light, but the flashlight does not.

20-21 Seeing the Sun

Your pinhole camera will show any large sunspots and can be used to watch eclipses safely. You can also use it to watch a transit of Venus, but you will have to wait until around December 10, 2117, for the next one!

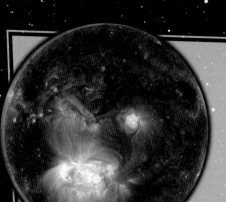

26–27 Different Suns?

When you compare images 2 and 3, you can see that the most magnetic areas in image 2 are in the same place as the sunspots in image 3. The fact that sunspots are magnetized was one of the most important discoveries in the history of solar observation.

32–33 In Transit

Venus and Mercury look like black silhouettes against the sun. If you look closely you can see that planet B looks larger than planet A. Planet B has to be Venus and planet A is Mercury. Not only is Venus bigger than Mercury, it is closer to Earth during transit.

40–41 What Is Equilibrium?

The balloon is a simple model to show the sun's equilibrium. The tightness of the balloon's skin is like the sun's gravity trying to squash it. The pressure inside the balloon is like the sun's energy trying to get out.

$$d = \sqrt{(x_2 - x_1) + (y_2 - y_1)^2}$$

GLOSSARY

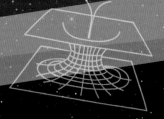

air pressure The push of air on the surface of objects.

atmosphere The blanket of gases around a planet.

atoms The smallest pieces you can split any elements into.

carbon A chemical element that diamonds and coal are made up of.

carbon dioxide A gas humans breathe out, which also occurs naturally.

civilizations Groups of people who organize their lives together, forming towns and cities, language, and culture.

comets Chunks of rock and ice in space, similar to asteroids.

density A measure of how packed together something is.

eclipse When the moon passes between Earth and the sun, or Earth passes between the moon and the sun.

eclipse glasses Special very dark glasses to view the sun without hurting your eyes.

electrons The negatively charged particles in an atom.

element The basic material from which everything is made.

emperors People who rule empires or are the heads of state in empires.

energy The ability to do work.

equator An imaginary line around the middle of a planet, moon, or star.

evaporates When a liquid turns into a gas.

evolved Gradually changed over time.

force A push or pull that can change the way things move.

fuel A substance that reacts, usually by burning, to release a lot of heat, which can be used to power things.

fuse To join together physically or chemically, usually to become one thing.

gamma rays Radiation with even shorter wavelengths than X-rays. Even more harmful to living things than X-rays.

gravity The pull that any object has on any other object. The bigger the object, or planet, the more gravity it has.

helium The second most common element in the universe and the second lightest gas.

horizon The strip of land we see in the distance just below the sky.

infrared Radiation we feel as heat.

inner solar system The part of the solar system that includes everything from the sun to the planet Mars.

magnetic field An invisible area of magnetic force around an object such as Earth.

matter Something that occupies space, has mass, and can exist as a solid, liquid, gas, or plasma.

nuclear weapon Explosive device that gets its force from nuclear reactions.

orbits Circular or oval paths around objects in space that are caused by the pull of the objects' gravity.

outer planets The planets Jupiter, Saturn, Uranus, and Neptune, which are found beyond the asteroid belt in the solar system.

oxygen A gas in Earth's atmosphere that living things need to breathe to survive.

penumbra Less-dark region around the center of a sunspot.

philosopher A person who is a thinker and teacher.

photosphere The topmost surface of the sun that we can see.

photosynthesis Process that plants use to convert carbon dioxide to oxygen, helping the plant grow with sunlight.

physicist A person who studies physics.

pole Point at the top or bottom of a planet, moon, or star around which everything spins.

THE SUN'S ENERGY

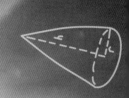

How much energy does the sun give out and how do we measure it? We use units such as feet, meters, miles, and kilometers to measure distance, and Fahrenheit and Celsius for temperature. To measure how much energy something has, we use a unit called the joule (J). One joule of energy is what you would need to lift a tomato an arm's length off the ground. The heat your body gives out is around 60 joules per second. If you eat a cheeseburger, the energy your body gains is around 2 million joules.

Changing Mass to Energy

When you eat the cheeseburger, you absorb some energy from its ingredients, but the mass of the cheeseburger is not destroyed. Instead it is converted into fats, sugars, and then your own waste. In 1905, Albert Einstein (1879–1955) proposed that the energy contained in matter was immense. What if you could change the matter in the cheeseburger into pure energy? Einstein's famous equation $E=mc^2$ describes what happens. If you want to know how much energy (E) something has, you have to multiply its mass (m) by c^2, which stands for the speed of light measured in meters per second, squared (multiplied by itself). Energy is expressed in joules, and mass in kilograms.

Einstein wrote more than 300 scientific papers during his career, but he is most remembered for his famous formula for converting mass into energy, $E=mc^2$.

prism Transparent device made of glass or plastic that can split light into different colors.

proton An atomic particle that has a positive electrical charge.

radiation Energy that travels at the speed of light. Includes visible light.

radio waves Radiation with much longer wavelengths than visible light. Can be used as a form of communication over long distances.

rainbow When it rains and is sunny at the same time, raindrops act as tiny prisms splitting sunlight into different colors.

red giant A giant star toward the end of its life that emits red light.

rotated Revolved or turned around a central axis, line, or point.

silhouette The solid, dark shape that is seen when someone or something has a bright light or pale background behind it.

solar activity sunspots, flares, and other storms on the sun.

solar system The sun, its planets and moons, asteroids and comets.

spectrum The range of radiation, from radio through visible to gamma rays.

supernovae Explosions at the end of massive stars' lives.

telegraph Old-fashioned method of communicating over long wires using electricity.

telescope A device that allows you to see objects in the sky by making them bigger.

ultraviolet (UV) Radiation with slightly shorter wavelengths than visible light. Naturally produced by the sun.

umbra Dark region in the center of a sunspot.

wavelength The distance between the crests of two waves, whether they are water, sound, or light waves.

X-rays Radiation with a shorter wavelength than visible light.

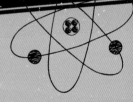

FURTHER READING

BOOKS

Garbe, Suzanne. *The Science Behind Wonders of the Sun*. New York, NY: Capstone, 2016.

Simon, Seymour. *The Sun*. Washington, D.C.: National Geographic School Pub, 2010.

Taylor-Butler, Christine. *The Sun* (A True Book). New York, NY: Scholastic, 2014.

WEBSITES

Due to the changing nature of Internet links, PowerKids Press has developed an online list of websites related to the subject of this book. This site is updated regularly. Please use this link to access the list: www.powerkidslinks.com/bass/oursun

INDEX